How we USE materials

Wool and Cotton

Rita Storey

W

First published in 2006 by
Franklin Watts
338 Euston Road
London NW1 3BH

Franklin Watts Australia
Hachette Children's Books
Level 17/207 Kent Street
Sydney NSW 2000

Art director: Jonathan Hair
Series designed and created for Franklin Watts by Painted Fish Ltd.
Designer: Rita Storey
Editor: Fiona Corbridge

Picture credits
Corbis/Jim Zukerman p. 16 (bottom); British Wool Marketing Board p. 8, p. 9, p. 11
(top); istockphoto.com p. 5, p. 7 (top), p. 11 (bottom), p. 12 (top), p. 13 (top), p. 15
(top), p. 16 (top), p. 17 (top and middle), p. 18, p. 19, p. 20, p. 21, p. 24, p. 25, p. 26
(top); SGS p. 6; Tudor Photography p. 3, p. 7 (bottom), p. 10, p. 12 (bottom),
p. 13 (bottom), p. 15 (middle and bottom), p. 17 (middle and bottom), p. 22, p. 23,
p. 26 (bottom), p. 27 (bottom).

Cover images: Tudor Photography, Banbury

ISBN-10: 0 7496 6461 4
ISBN-13: 978 0 7496 6461 9
Dewey classification: 677

A CIP catalogue record for this book is available from the British Library.

Printed in China

Contents

Words in **bold** are
in the glossary.

What is wool?

Wool is a **natural material** that comes from animals such as sheep and goats. Wool is useful for making **fabrics** and clothes.

Wool is made of long hairs called fibres. You can see one of them in this close-up photo. Wool fibres have **scales** and are bendy. The bends in the fibres make wool stretchy.

We use wool to make clothes such as jumpers and coats.

We also use wool for carpets and rugs.

Fabrics made from wool can be thick and hairy like this scarf.

Wool fabrics can also be thin and fine like this baby's suit.

7

Where does wool come from?

Most wool comes from sheep. It is the hair sheep grow to keep warm. It is called a **fleece**.

In the spring, a sheep's fleece is cut off. This is called **shearing**. Shearing a sheep does not hurt it. The wool soon grows back again.

A sheep's fleece is full of dirt. Before it can be used, the wool has to be washed in hot, soapy water. Then it is combed to get rid of knots.

The wool fibres are twisted and pulled into a thin thread called **yarn**. Different thicknesses of yarn are used to make different types of wool fabric.

Wool keywords
Fleece
Combed
Shearing
Yarn

Wool in the home

We use wool for things in our homes because it feels soft and can keep us warm.

- Wool yarn can be made into fabric by **weaving** threads of yarn together. One set of threads goes over and under another set. Blankets are often **woven**.

Carpets are made from wool because wool is soft and warm to walk on. Wool is sometimes mixed with a hard-wearing material called **nylon**. Wool and nylon carpets last longer than those made only of wool.

Wool keywords
Soft
Warm
Stretchy
Woven

Wool fabric is slightly stretchy and does not **crease**. This makes it a useful material for covering chairs and sofas.

Wool to wear

Wool is warm, lightweight and does not crease very easily. It is a useful material for making clothes.

Knitting is a way of making fabric by joining up lots of loops of yarn. It can be done by hand with knitting needles, or on a machine.

● **Woollen** yarn can be woven into cloth to make fabrics such as **tartan**.

● Natural wool is cream, grey, black or brown. Wool can be coloured by dipping it into **chemicals** called **dyes**. This jumper is knitted from different coloured wool.

Wool keywords
Knitting
Lightweight
Dyes

13

Felt

If wool fibres are **steamed** and pressed together, they make a material called **felt**.

Felt can be **moulded** into different shapes to make hats.

You can cut felt into shapes too. This pincushion is decorated with a green felt shape.

A type of felt called **baize** is used to make the surface of **pool tables**.

The tip of a felt-tipped pen can be made of wool felt.

Wool felt is used to make the outside of tennis balls.

Wool keywords

Steamed
Felt
Baize

15

What is cotton?

Cotton is a natural material that comes from the cotton plant. It is a useful material because it can be made into fabric.

The cotton from a cotton plant is made of fibres. This is a cotton fibre shown very close up.

We use cotton fabric to make clothes such as shirts and dresses. We also use it for sheets, tea towels and curtains.

Some cotton fabric is thick, strong and hard-wearing. It is used to make **overalls**.

Cotton fabric can also be thin, light and fine, like this handkerchief.

Cotton keywords
Strong
Hard-wearing
Thin

Where does cotton come from?

Cotton fabric is made from the fibres that surround the seeds of the cotton plant.

The cotton is ready when the seed pod opens to show the fluffy white cotton fibres inside.

The cotton is picked by hand or with machines.

A machine called a **gin** separates the fibres from the seeds. The fibres are cleaned and tied together in **bales**.

Cotton fibres are twisted together and pulled into long, thin ropes called yarn.

Cotton yarn is knitted or woven together and made into cotton fabric.

Cotton keywords

Fibres
Yarn
Fabric

Cotton in the home

Cotton is useful in our homes because it is hard-wearing. It can be washed often and still looks good.

Cotton **absorbs** water so it is a good material for making towels. The cotton yarn is made into lots of loops to absorb more water.

Bedlinen, such as pillowcases, is often made of cotton. It keeps you cool and comfortable in bed.

Cotton is easy to wash. It is used to make tablecloths because they need washing a lot.

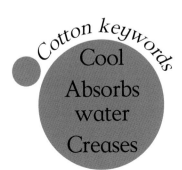

Cotton creases when it is washed. It can be treated to help it stay smooth so it needs less ironing.

Cotton keywords
Cool
Absorbs water
Creases

Cotton to wear

We use cotton to make clothes because it keeps us cool in hot weather and it looks nice.

Natural cotton is cream in colour. We can make it different colours by dipping it into chemicals called dyes.

Cotton fabric can be **printed** with patterns before it is made up into clothes.

Cotton yarn can be made into cloth by knitting it. Knitted cotton is stretchy. We make T-shirts from it.

Denim is a strong, thick cotton fabric, which lasts a long time. We use it to make jeans and overalls.

Cotton keywords

Dye
Denim
Printed
Knitted

Cotton outside

Cotton is very hard-wearing but it soaks up water. It can be treated with chemicals to make it waterproof, so it can be used outside.

Thick waterproof cotton fabric is sometimes used to make tents and **caravan awnings**.

● Chair covers and deckchairs are made of thick cotton fabric. It is strong enough to hold a person's weight.

● These sun umbrellas are made of thick cotton fabric. They will last for a long time.

● *Cotton keywords*
Chemicals
Waterproof
Thick

Other uses of cotton

Cotton is used in lots of ways to make different things. Sometimes you cannot tell they have cotton in them.

● Cotton is used to stuff cushions, mattresses and duvets.

● Teabags are made of cotton. They are fine and light, and cheap to make.

Cotton is used in paper to make it strong and hard-wearing. Banknotes have cotton fibres in them.

Cotton wool is made of soft cotton fibres. It is cheap to make and buy, so we can throw it away when it has been used.

Cotton keywords

Cheap
Hard-wearing

Glossary

Absorbs Takes in liquid. A towel absorbs water.

Baize A felt-like material used for covering pool tables.

Bales Bundles of materials tied together with string.

Bedlinen Sheets, duvet covers and pillowcases.

Caravan awning A frame covered with canvas (a type of cotton) on the side of a caravan, used as an extra room.

Chemicals Special substances used to do many jobs, including making dyes and waterproofing.

Crease A fold or wrinkle in fabric; or to become folded or wrinkled.

Dyes Substances used to colour fabric.

Fabrics Types of cloth made by weaving, felting or knitting fibres together.

Felt A fabric made of matted cotton fibres.

Fleece The wool coat of a sheep or similar animal.

Gin A machine that separates the seeds of the cotton plant from the cotton fibres.

Knitting A way of making fabric by joining up lots of loops of yarn.

Moulded Made into a different shape.

Natural material Comes from the Earth, plants or animals.

Nylon A man-made material made from chemicals. It is used for clothing.

Overalls Loose-fitting clothes worn over regular clothing to protect them from dirt.

Pool tables Heavy tables that the game of pool is played on.

Printed Marked with a pattern.

Scales Overlapping layers.

Shearing Cutting off the fleece from a sheep.

Steamed Heated over boiling water.

Tartan A traditional woollen cloth woven in coloured checks and lines.

Weaving/woven A way of making yarn into cloth using two sets of threads, which go over and under each other.

Woollen Made out of wool.

Yarn A long thread made from the fibres of wool or cotton, which is used to make fabric.

Index